THE WOLFHOUND GUIDE
TO
Hurling

THE WOLFHOUND GUIDE
TO
Hurling

BRENDAN FULLAM

WOLFHOUND PRESS

Published in 1999 by
Wolfhound Press Ltd
68 Mountjoy Square
Dublin 1, Ireland
Tel: (353-1) 874 0354
Fax: (353-1) 872 0207

British Library Cataloguing in Publication Data
A catalogue record for this book is available from the British Library

ISBN 0-86327-724-1

10 9 8 7 6 5 4 3 2 1

Action Photos Courtesy Inpho Photography (pages 8, 34, 40, 41, 45, 60, 64, 78)
Line Illustrations: Ann Fallon
Cover Illustration: Nicola Emoe
Cover Design: Slick Fish Design, Dublin
Typesetting: Wolfhound Press
Printed by Edelvives, Spain

Contents

Dedicated with deep appreciation
and fond memories
to Mary
the mother who reared me

Chapter One

The Beginning

Hurling at its best is a beautifully balanced blend of silken skills and fierce man-to-man combat, a spectacle of sport that beggars description.

Paddy Downey

To find the origins of the game we must look back into the twilight of fable. It is arguably the oldest field game in the world. Reference is found in literature to a game between the Tuatha de Danann and the Firbolgs around the year BC1272.

The Tuatha de Danann belonged to the Spiritual World. They inspired their people to believe in the spiritual side of their nature. They worshipped the sun, moon and stars, together with the elements — earth, fire and water. The Firbolgs, on the other hand, believed in the power of physical force. They were an earthy race. Primary for them was the urge to gain supremacy over any and all opposition. They liked to conquer.

The Tuatha de Danann and the Firbolgs belonged to the Bronze Age. We are told that the Firbolgs won the hurling game. But do we really know? It was the goals and points of the physical world meaured against the goals and points of the spiritual world. What or where is the common denominator that evaluates the two? The search is an eternal one.

Oh God! please grant that when this life I'll yield;
That in Heaven you'll have a hurling field.
With goal posts white and a green field grand —
and sunny days and a good pipe band.

from *The Hurler's Wish* by J. Ryan

Chapter Two

The Myth and Legend

In ancient times when Eire reigned
A Nation great and grand,
When Oscar's and Cú Chulainn's fame
Was spread throughout the land;
On Tailteann plain with might and main,
In contests fiercely drawn,
What else could grace the pride of place,
But the well-grained ash camán?

Phil O'Neill
'Sliabh Ruadh'

The game of hurling is very much part of Irish myth and legend. Most famous of the stories is from the Red Branch Knights (An Craobh Ruadh), and is about Cú Chulainn. It is recounted in The Táin and set in the Iron Age — the age of the Celtic people. It was a time when a code of honour was central to behaviour — you lived honourably; you played honourably. It was an age of chivalry.

In Cú Chulainn is epitomised all that is daring, dashing, flamboyant and gallant in the ancient game.

Legend tells us that Cú Chulainn — then known as Setanta — left his father's home in Dundalk, County Louth, to visit his uncle, King Conor MacNessa, who resided in Eamhain Macha, about a mile to the west of the present city of Armagh. To shorten the journey he took with him his hurley and sliotar. As he set off, he pucked the ball up into the air ahead of himself. Fleet of foot, he ran and met the sliotar as it descended, sending it upwards and onwards again. And so the process continued for the entire journey, with the young Setanta displaying as he travelled all the qualities of a class hurler — speed, skill, accuracy, stamina, precision, and first-touch perfection.

In due course he reached his destination, still full of vim, vigour and vitality, only to discover that his uncle had gone to a celebration at the Dún of his friend Culann. On to the Dún went Setanta. But a shock awaited him there. The Dún was guarded by a fierce hound. Snarling, and with white teeth flashing, he thundered towards Setanta. With a coolness born of the supreme confidence of a master, Setanta steadied, took aim and sank the sliotar in the throat of the hound. Its feet buckled as it fell to the ground, howling and shrieking and wailing — *ag béicig, ag scréachaig agus ag olagón.*

Those at the feast heard the commotion and the awful shrieks of the dying hound. They emerged to witness the final choking moments — none more horrified than Culann.

Culann was a blacksmith. The hound guarded his Dún. Now he had no guard. But honour and chivalry prevailed.

Conor MacNessa proclaimed that since Setanta had slain the hound he would now take the place of the hound — adding that as he was good enough to kill the guard-dog, he must certainly be good enough to replace it. And so Setanta was re named Cú-Chulainn — the hound of Culann. He is immortalised in legend.

Then there is the story of King Labraidh Loinsigh. Labraidh was born with two afflictions. First of all, he had horse's ears; these were such an acute embarrassment to him that he always kept them covered. He was also dumb. Dumb, that is, until one day when playing a game of hurling he got a fierce belt on the shin. So great was the pain that it enabled him to shout aloud in agony. The words and expletives uttered have been lost and buried in the mists of time — just as well, perhaps. His speech defect was cured. Word spread throughout his kingdom, and the game of hurling had bestowed upon it a special place of honour. The problem of the ears, however, was not solved.

From the earliest times the Irish people have dearly loved a contest. Parish, barony and county have called forth remarkable loyalty in the Irish soul. The rules of hurling have always permitted an exciting contest. Like a national magnet, it has attracted people of all ages. The game has ever been embedded deep in the Irish psyche.

In ancient Ireland, Aonach Tailteann, named after Taillte, wife of the last King of the Firbolgs, was held on the first day of August — Lá Lughnasa. The men of Ireland gathered and indulged in such sports as chariot-racing, horse-racing and hurling.

The epic of Diarmaid and Grainne gives clear evidence of the antiquity of hurling, and the esteem in which it was held in ancient Ireland is greater than for any game in world literature. Grainne fell in love with Diarmaid as she watched him hurling — a goal he scored sealed her love.

Skill with the camán was part of the school curriculum — it was a preparation for manly skills with arms. The young princes carried camáns with bands of gold or silver according to rank.

In the Brehon laws, which preceded feudalism in Ireland, we find sophisticated provisions to compensate the families of any man killed by a hurley or a hurling ball. King Cahir the Great of Tailteann left fifty brass hurleys and fifty brass hurling balls in his will.

In modern times, Charles Kickham's Matt the Thresher in *Knocknagow* and Canon Sheehan's Terence Casey in *Glenanaar* are but recreations of the hurling heroes of Oisín's time.

Of course, it must be borne in mind that a determined attempt to suppress all things Irish, including hurling, was made when the Statutes of Kilkenny came into existence in 1366. However, it would take more than written words, even if they did carry the weight of royal power at the time, to rob the Gael of the sublime gift of hurling.

Without going into the background of Terence Casey — alias 'The Yank' — the game of hurling as related in *Glenanaar* is worth recalling:

> *It was a Sunday afternoon in the late summer. There was a tournament in the Park. In past times it used to be called a hurling-match, but we are going ahead in Ireland, and we call things now by their proper names. It was a big affair — the culmination and critical finish of all the many local trials of strength that had taken place in the past year. It was the final 'try' for the County championship between the Cork 'Shandons', and our own brave 'Skirmishers'. There was a mighty crowd assembled. Sidecars, waggonettes, traps of every shape and hue and form, from the farmer's cart with the heavy quilt to the smart buggy of the merchant, brought in all the afternoon a great concourse of people, who were anxious to put down the Sunday evening in the best possible manner by witnessing this great joust of Irish athletes....*

...It was to be a trial of strength between two nearly matched clubs, in which grit, and wind, and pluck, and muscle, and science were to be put to their final test.

At three o'clock the teams were called to their places by their respective captains. There was a brief consultation with the referee, a coin was flung into the air, sides were taken, the winners turning their backs to the wind, and in a moment, one could only see that ball tossed hither and thither in the struggle, and a confused mass of men and camáns, as they fought fiercely for victory and the tide of the battle rolled uncertain here and there across the field. And the combatants were curiously silent. This, too, is a modern characteristic, and a wholesome one. Instead of the whoops and yells of olden times, the words of fierce encouragement or expostulation, the cry of victory, and the curse of defeat, one only saw the set faces and the flying figures, the victory snatched out of the hands of one, the defeat of the other retrieved, and the swift, tumultuous passion that swayed these young athletes as they strained every nerve in the all-important struggle for victory.

Not a word broke from that whirling mass, as the heavy ball leaped hither and thither, tossed by the camáns from hand to hand, or rolled swiftly over the level grass, as some young athlete, with the fleetness of a deer, tapped it on before him, until he brought it within reach of the coveted goal. You heard only the patter of feet, the light or heavy tap-tap-tap on the ball, the crack of the camáns as they crossed in the air above or on the grass beneath; and now and again the screams of women and girls, who stampeded wildly when the ball was driven into their midst, and the fierce flying combatants, with heaving breasts and starting eyes, forgot their chivalry and carried the tumult of battle right in amongst their excited sisters. Indeed, the whole excitement seemed to be limited to the spectators, who cheered and lamented, encouraged or rebuked the silent athletes on whom the honour of the flag depended. One alone amidst the din and tumult of the field maintained a stoical composure, and that was 'the Yank'. He stood apart and watched the strife, as impassive as an Indian chief, apparently regardless as to which side victory swayed; and altogether taking but an academic and far-off interest in the entire affair.

At half-past four the teams were almost on a tie, the 'Skirmishers' having two goals to their credit, and the 'Shandons' one goal and some points. The final tussle was just about to come off, when it was announced that the local captain had been taken suddenly ill, and had been ordered off the field. There was consternation in the ranks of the 'Skirmishers', Just on the point of victory, their hopes were dashed to the ground. They held a long and eager consultation; and finally decided to enlist one or other of the spectators, who had been members of the Club, but not picked men. These shook their heads. The issue was too important. They would not take the responsibility. Five o'clock was near; and the referee was about to give his final decision in favour of the

*strangers, when, to the astonishment of everyone, 'the Yank',
throwing away a half-burned cigar, and calmly divesting himself of coat and waistcoat, which he carefully rolled up
and placed in the hands of a spectator, came forward, took
up a camán, tested it, as if it were a Toledo blade, by leaning all
his weight upon it, and said in an accent of cool
indifference:*

'Let me take a hand: I guess I can manage it.'

*There was a general laugh. The 'Shandons' were delighted.
They noticed the grey hairs in his head and beard. The
'Skirmishers' demurred; but one wise fellow, who had
been studying the splendid build of 'the Yank', winked and said:*

'Yes, we'll take him. Put him right inside the goal.'

*The excitement rose rapidly with this new event. The
disabled Captain heard of it, and insisted upon being taken
back to see the issue. No matter if he died on the field of battle!
'Where can man die better?' etc., etc. The ball was once more
tossed high, the victory swayed from one side to the other; the
cheers rose wildly and voluminously from the adherents of
both teams; until, at last, the 'Shandons', pressing home for victory, drove the ball right under 'the Yank's' legs. The foremost
champion, rushing forward to get it through the goal, found
himself, he knew not how, about twenty feet away from the
ball; and then it seemed as if a cyclone had struck the field. At
least, a straight path was cut through the swaying, confused
mass of the combatants, who in some mysterious way yielded*

right and left. Disregarding all modern rules and regulations, 'the Yank' had struck straight before him; and with his powerful arms and shoulders had cut his way as clean as a swathe of ripe corn is levelled by the teeth of the mowing-machine in the early harvest time. He swept along quite close to where I was standing; and once I heard him panting: T'ainim an diaoul. Then I knew he was Irish; and my heart went out to him. A few cries of 'A foul! A foul!' were raised; but they were hushed into ignominious silence by the plaudits of the crowd, whose feelings of respectful aversion were suddenly converted into a paroxysm of unstinted admiration. 'Go it, Yank!' 'Cheers for the "Stars and Stripes"!' 'Give them "Hail Columbia", old fellow!' echoed on every side, until the whole mad tumult culminated in a wild Irish cheer, as the ball flew swiftly over the heads of the rival combatants, and, despite the frantic efforts of the goal-keeper on the 'Shandons" side, passed out gaily through the gates of the goal. Just as the 'Yank' struck the ball the blow that gained the victory, there was a wild, mad rush toward him; and under its weight he was flung down, whilst the whole human mass squirmed over him. There was a wild shout of indignation from the field, for he had suddenly become their hero; and it seemed like revenge for defeat. When they were raised, one by one, 'the Yank' was unable to lift himself. A hundred willing hands offered to help him; and there were some angry threats toward those who had felled him. A few distinctively Gaelic questions were also put:

'You're not dead, are you?'

'Wal, no,' he said, leisurely, but with a gesture of pain, 'but I guess there are broken bones somewhere, anyhow.'

He was gently raised on a stretcher, and carried in triumph from the field. As the bearers were passing out the front gate, the captain of the local team came forward and proffered his thanks for the assistance given. He looked wretchedly ill, but he thought he had his duty to perform.

'Wal,' said the Yank, in his own cool way, 'I guess we did lick them. But, young man, you go home, and liquor up as fast as you can.'

Half-way down the street, an old man, looking sideways at the hero, said aloud:

'Begobs, there was nothin' seen like it since Casey the Hurler's time.'

The Yank raised himself with difficulty, and fixing his eyes on the old man, he said:

'Say that agin, Mister!'

'I say,' repeated the old man, somewhat embarrassed now, 'that there was nothin' seen like that since Terence Casey single-handed bate the parishes of Ardpatrick and Glenroe.'

'That was a long time ago, I guess,' said the Yank, leaning back helplessly again.

extract from *Glenanaar* by Canon Sheehan

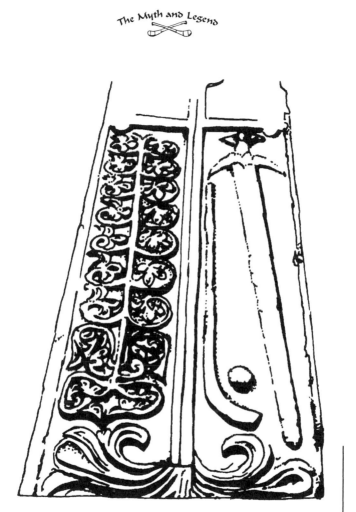

Fifteenth-century grave slab depicting hurley and sliotar.

The Hurler

Upon his native sward the hurler stands
To play the ancient pastime of the Gael,
And all the heroes famed of Innisfail
Are typified in him — I see the bands
Of the Craobh Ruadh applauding with their hands,
The Fianna shouting over Clui-Mail,
Oisín and Finn with eager faces pale,
Caoiltí and Goll are there from fairy lands.

And fierce Cú Chulainn comes, his Godlike face,
With yearning wild to grip in hand once more
The lithe camán and drive the hurtling ball.
In Walsh's, Kelleher's, and Semple's grace
He sees again his glorious youth of yore,
And mourns his dead compeers and Ferdia's fall.

Rev. James B. Dollard, D.Litt.

Chapter Three

Evolution of the Game

 PART ONE

'So long and so unsullied has the game been handed down from sire to son that the very parish soil is permeated with the hurling spirit.'

Carbery

Hurling has evolved over the centuries. Had it stood still, it would have died.

Instance the story of The Táin. No mention is made of frees or fouls or referees or side-line cuts. Strength, speed, stamina, skill, dexterity and endurance would appear to have been the key qualities.

The Norman conquest, which began in 1169, was followed in time by English rule. Laws were made under the new régime, with a view to banning and suppressing the game. Most notable of these were the Statutes of Kilkenny, 1366. All of these attempts failed.

An rud a beirtear sa cnámh is deacair scarúint leis sa bhfuil.

That which is innate and borne in the spirit can never be suppressed.

Throughout the eighteenth century the game flourished, chiefly because of patronage by the landlords, who sponsored teams and organised games with other landlords. They even participated themselves. Of course, they had their own reasons for promoting the game. It provided wonderful entertainment for them and for their tenants. It also created a bond with the tenants and ensured friendly encounters with them. Moreover, it produced heroes and bestowed status on the victors. Wagers were part and parcel of the encounters, and added to the enjoyment of the occasion.

The following appeared in the *Dublin Flying Post* on 26 June 1708:

> On St Swithen's Day, about three in the afternoon, will be a Hurling Match over the Curragh, between 30 men from each side of the Liffey, for thirty shillings. A barrel of ale, tobacco, and pipes will be given to the hurlers.

The *Cork Evening Post* carried the following notice on 4 September 1769:

> A bet of 300 guineas, a cold dinner and a Ball at night for the Ladies, to be hurled for on Friday 9th inst., by 21 married men and 21 bachelors, on the Green of Ardfinnan in the County of Tipperary.
>
> N.B. None admitted to play but the Gentlemen of the Baronies of Iffa and Offa in the said county.

In the book *Famous Tullaroan*, Peter Holohan in an article on hurling wrote the following:

In the eighteenth century it was probably the most popular pastime in the country. The Lord Lieutenant, the pillar of the ruling British government at the time, was a regular attender at hurling matches and described them as the most exciting in Europe.

Other enthusiastic supporters of the game were the Countess of Westmoreland and the Countess of Northumberland and the latter is reputed to have wagered 1,000 guineas on a game between Galway and Tipperary played at Banagher.

The game was played in September 1773. The Countess of Northumberland described a hurling game she saw at the Curragh as 'the most noble and manly exercise in the world'.

About three hundred years ago Sir Caesar Colclough of Tintern in South Wexford took a team of twenty-one of his tenants to Cornwall to play the men of that territory. The Cornish men expected to triumph. It is said that Colclough gave his men a glass of whiskey apiece and told them to tie yellow kerchiefs around their middles so that they would easily recognise each other on the field. The men of Wexford won, and, in so doing, so impressed King William and his wife, who were present that day, that they were heard to shout, 'Well done, Yellow Bellies, Fine Fellows, Yellow Bellies.' The name stuck and Wexfordmen are proud of its origin.

Lecky's *History of Ireland 1783–1850* carried the following description of a game of hurling:

The great game in Kerry and indeed throughout the South is the game of 'Hurley' — a game rather rare, although not unknown in England. It is a fine manly exercise, with sufficient of danger to produce excitement; and is indeed, par excellence, the game of the peasantry of Ireland. To be an expert hurler, a man must possess athletic powers of no ordinary character; he must have a quick eye, a ready hand, and a strong arm; he must be a good runner, a skilful wrestler, and withal, patient as well as resolute....

The forms of the game are these: The players, sometimes to the number of fifty or sixty, being chosen for each side, they are arranged (usually bare-foot) in two opposing ranks, with their hurleys crossed, to await the tossing-up of the ball, the wickets or goals being previously fixed at the extremities of the hurling-green, which, from the nature of the play, is required to be a level extensive plain.... A person is chosen to throw up the ball, which is done as straight as possible, when the whole party, withdrawing their hurleys, stand with them elevated, to receive and strike it in its descent; now comes the crash of mimic war, hurleys rattle against hurleys — the ball is struck and restruck, often for several minutes, without advancing much nearer to either goal; and when someone is lucky enough to get a clear 'puck' at it, it is sent flying over the field. It is now followed by the entire party at their utmost speed; the men grapple, wrestle, and toss each other with amazing agility, neither victor nor vanquished waiting to take breath, but following the course of the rolling and flying prize; the best runners match each other, and keep almost shoulder to shoulder through the play, and the best wrestlers keep as close on them as possible to arrest or impede their progress. The ball must not be taken from the ground by the hand; and the tact and skill shown in taking it on the point of the hurley, and running with it half the length of the field, and when too closely pressed, striking it towards the goal, is a matter of astonishment to those who are but slightly acquainted with the play.

At the goal is the chief brunt of the battle. The goal-keepers receive the prize, and are opposed by those set over them; the struggle is tremendous — every power of strength and skill is exerted; while the parties from opposite sides of the field run at full speed to support their men engaged in the conflict; then the tossing and straining is at its height: the men often lying in dozens side by side on the grass, while the ball is returned by some strong arm again, flying above their heads, towards the goal. Thus for hours has the contention been carried on, and frequently the darkness of night arrests the game without giving victory to either side. It is often attended with danger-ous, and sometimes with fatal, results.

Matches are made, sometimes between different townlands or parishes, sometimes by barony against barony, and not unfrequently county against county: when the 'crack men' from the most distant parts are selected, and the interest excit-ed is proportionately great. About half a century ago, there was a great match played in the Phoenix Park, Dublin, between the Munstermen and the men of Leinster. It was got up by the then Lord Lieutenant and other sporting noblemen, and was attended by all the nobility and gentry belonging to the Vice-Regal Court, and the beauty and fashion of the Irish capital and its vicinity. The victory was contended for a long time, with varied success; and at last it was decided in favour of the

Munstermen, by one of that party, running with the ball on the point of his hurley and striking it through the open windows of the Vice-Regal carriage, and by that manoeuvre baffling the vigilance of the Leinster goalsmen, and driving it in triumph through the goal.

The rising of the United Irishmen in 1798 and the terror caused among the nobles by the French Revolution resulted in the landlords withdrawing their patronage. This and other factors — among them the potato failure of 1845 and 1846, as a result of which one million of the population died and a further million emigrated — caused the game to go seriously into decline in the nineteenth century, and at the time of the foundation of the GAA in 1884 the state of the game was so perilous that Michael Cusack's chief clarion cry was 'Bring back the hurling'. And he did.

Hurling survives and is indestructible because of its stern naked grandeur.

Carbery

 **PART 2**

Con Houlihan, author and journalist, in his Foreword to *Legends of the Ash* made the following observations:

There were two forms of hurling in Ireland: Winter hurling was played with a narrow stick and a hard ball; Summer hurling was played with a broad-bladed stick and a soft ball. You weren't allowed to handle the ball in the former; it was very much a feature of the latter.

Michael Cusack pondered long and deeply when the time came to decide which version he would make official; he chose the Summer version probably because it was more widespread at the time and was more attractive.

Winter hurling survived in the odd nook and occasional cranny; it was played in south west Kerry until about forty years ago, mainly on the roads and with improvised camáns. It is probably fair to say that Summer hurling was played on the better land and by the better-off people — the Winter game was favoured more by the working class.

It was played too in our part of Kerry, a few miles north of Castle Island. There was little traffic in the War years; we engaged in fierce battles on the Dublin Road — for a ball we used the bottom half of a small polish box.

When writing on the same theme in *The Tribune Magazine* of 16 October 1994, Kevin Whelan had this to say:

By the 18th Century there were two principal and regionally distinct versions of the game. 'Commons' was akin to the modern Scottish game of shinty; it did not allow handling of the ball which was wooden and hard; it used a narrow-bladed crocked stick. A Winter game, it was played by both Presbyterians and Catholics and it was confined to the Northern third of the island, especially Antrim, Derry and Donegal. 'Baire' or 'Iomán', the second version, was by contrast a Summer game of Southern Provenance. The soft animal hair ball (the sliotar) could be handled or carried on the hurl which was flat and round headed.

Unlike 'commons' this version was extensively patronised by the landed gentry as a spectator and gambling sport....

Michael Cusack was determined to create a sporting organisation which suited the Irish rural poor especially the labourer, artisan and small farmer. Gaelic games would emancipate them from the tyranny of the existing athletic clubs. Cusack's genius was to meet this social need while retaining the territorial allegiances which typified the older games....

Its social base came especially from journalists, school teachers, priests and publicans.... Hurling gradually became what Cusack had envisaged — a National fine art form.... But this very strength of hurling was also its weakness. Because a highly complex array of skills are required for proficiency, hurling requires sympathetic nurture at the childhood stage, when the hurl must be grafted on as a natural extension of the hand.... Hurling is an intensely regional game, nourished in its traditional heartlands where the field of experience was also a field of dreams. At moments of peak intensity, the great game of hurling — like any great art form — abolished time and established memory.

 **PART 3**

THE SCORING AREA

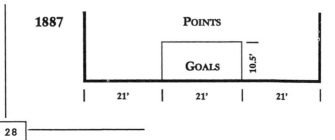

1887   POINTS

GOALS   10.5'

21'   21'   21'

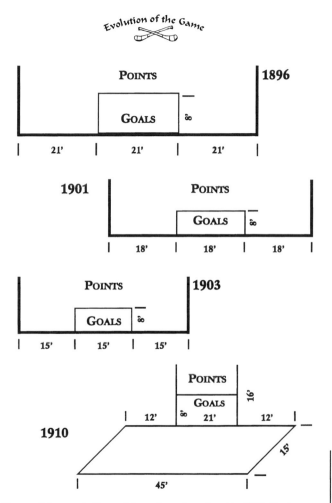

The parallelogram in front of the goal was introduced in 1910. Goals scored were allowed only when opposing players were not therein before the arrival of the sliotar.

TEAM NUMBERS AND LINE-OUT FORMATION

At the time of the first championship in 1887 teams consisted of 21 aside. This continued until 1891. The following diagram shows the format.

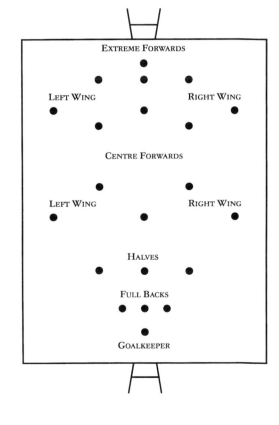

In 1892, at the Congress held in Thurles on 13 January, teams were reduced to 17 aside and this continued until 1912.

The manner in which teams lined-out under this system is illustrated in the diagram below.

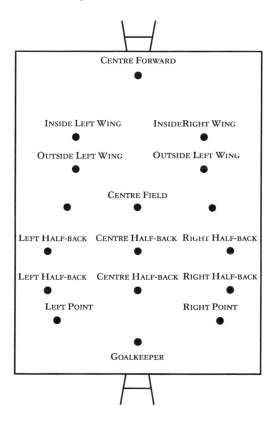

CENTRE FORWARD

INSIDE LEFT WING   INSIDERIGHT WING

OUTSIDE LEFT WING   OUTSIDE LEFT WING

CENTRE FIELD

LEFT HALF-BACK CENTRE HALF-BACK RIGHT HALF-BACK

LEFT HALF-BACK CENTRE HALF-BACK RIGHT HALF-BACK

LEFT POINT   RIGHT POINT

GOALKEEPER

A further modification took place in 1913 when, following a decision at Central Council on 23 March, teams were reduced to 15 aside. This has continued up to the present day. The diagram shows how they line out.

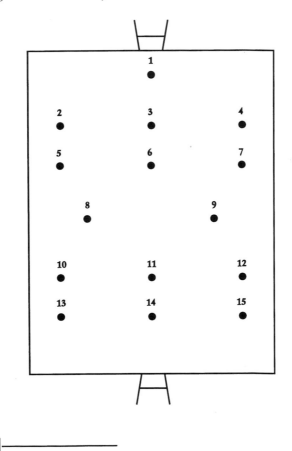

SCORE VALUES

From 1887 to 1891 inclusive, no number of points equalled a goal.

For the period 1892 to 1895 inclusive, a goal was made equal to 5 points, as decided at the Congress held in Thurles.

In 1896, at the Congress in Thurles on 10 May, the value of a goal was reduced to 3 points, and that position has remained unchanged up to the present time.

MODERNISATION

By 1913, the structure that obtains today was agreed:

— Teams consisted of fifteen aside.

— A goal was equal to three points.

— The scoring area was as modified in 1910.

It is interesting to note that at the time of the very first championship in 1887 a forfeit point was allowed if a player sent the sliotar over his own end line, wide of the posts. Five forfeit points were equal to one point.

This was changed at Congress in 1888. The forfeit point was abolished. A 40-yards free was awarded instead to the opposing team.

Initially, this was allowed only if a player deliberately sent it over his own end line, wide of the posts. Inevitably, it led to disputes, and the rule was altered, so that if the last person to play or touch or be touched by the sliotar caused it to cross his own end line, the free was awarded.

Some time later, the 40-yards free was changed to a 50-yards free, and in 1910 it was further changed to a 70-yards free.

Chapter Four

The Game and its Requisites

The Irish word for hurling is *iomáin* or *iománaíocht*, which means the art of driving, hurling, tossing forward, pressing or urging forward.

The Irish word for a hurler, based on the same root, is *iománaí*; the plural is *iománaithe*.

Ar dhroim an domhain níl radharc is áille,
Ná triocha fear ag bualadh báire.

In the whole world there is no more beautiful sight
Than thirty men playing hurling.

The game is played with a hard ball, called a *sliotar*. It has cork at its centre. This is covered with layers of thread. Its outer covering is two strips of pigskin leather, shaped so that, when placed together and wax-stitched, they form a sphere and encase the cork and thread. Nowadays, the leather is treated to make it water-resistant. Decades ago, before the water-resistant treatment became available, the sliotar got very sodden in wet conditions, which of course made it heavier and shortened the distance it could be driven. The circumference of the modern sliotar is approximately 9.5 inches, considerably smaller than its predecessors.

Oh for the clash of the ash so sweet,
The flying ball and the hurlers fleet.

Carbery

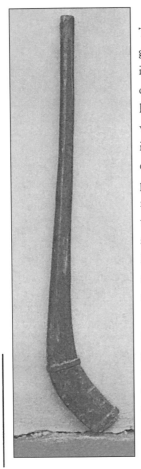

The implement used in playing the game is called a hurley. The Irish word is *camán*, meaning a stick with a crooked head — and that's what a hurley is. It is made from ash — a wood that is pliable and ideal for resisting fierce man-to-man clashes in exchanges for supremacy. The lower portion of the camán is called the *bas*, meaning something that is flat. It is with the bas of the hurley that the sliotar is struck. Every player likes to have a hurley where the grain of the ash travels down the handle and curves naturally with the shape of the bas.

Camáns vary in length depending on the size of the player. A general guide is that when the hurley is stood upwards, on the ground and against the leg, it should reach the hip bone of the user.

Hurley used by the Kerry team to win the 1891 All-Ireland Senior title.

The author with President Mary Robinson during a presentation of a modern hurley and sliotar to the President.

Players become very attached to their camáns; a hurler sees his camán as really an extension of himself. When it gets broken, he feels he has lost a close possession.

The mountain ash had its mystic place in ancient Irish rites. Fashioned as a lithe camán, it is the symbol of physical fitness and national integrity today. The grip of native ash draws impressionable young hearts back to the soil and atmosphere of gaeldom.

Celt

'Twas coming from the Fair of Ross, I spied that bend of growing ash,
And swore I'd cut the makings true, before the night was done;
Tho' tyrants held the woodland then, close guarded by Black Tady Nash,
I shouldered home the 'soople' tree before the morning sun.

Carbery
'The Old Hurler's Song to His Ash'

Oh! Cut me a hurl from the mountain ash
That weathered many a gale,
And my stroke will be lithe as the lightning's flash
That leaps from the thunder's flail;
And my feet shall be swift as the white spin-drift
On the bay in the wintry weather,
As we run in line through the glad sunshine
On the trail of the whirling leather.

Crawford Neil
'The Song of the Hurler'

Chapter Five

The Attractiveness of the Game

From time to time foreigners from many countries, west and east, have had the pleasure of witnessing hurling at Croke Park and Semple Stadium, Thurles. They have all marvelled at the game — the speed, skill, courage, seeming reckless abandon, fierce man-to-man combat and remarkable level of sportsmanship.

One of the great strengths of the game lies in the fact that it is amateur. All players are on an equal footing. They play for the sheer love of the game, 'for the honour of the little village'. They receive no payment whatsoever. But nowadays, with so many counter-attractions and competition from other sports, there is a growing awareness that players must be treated well and compensated for expenses incurred in travelling to training sessions.

Why is hurling such a powerful spectacle? I long ago came to the conclusion that its magic lies in the fact that it is totally devoid of inhibitions. In rugby and soccer you have the offside rule. In hockey you can't raise the stick above a certain height, and you can use only one side of the stick. Hurling is free of such rules. You can swing, left or right, on a coming ball. You can pull, with or against, in the air or on the ground.

You can meet the ball on the drop — with or against. You can grab it in flight. It may be lifted from the ground with the hurley and taken in the hand, or may be lifted and struck in the one movement. The one restriction is that it may not be picked off the ground by the hand.

The game is, of course, a reflection of the Irish temperament. It satisfies the spirit and the body. There is a hosting, a gathering of kindred spirits — kindred spirits who are passionate, yet discerning enough to admire the brilliance of friend and foe. They mingle and come together to see non-stop action and excitement — swaying, lurching fortunes; never-say-die spirit; drama; the clash and sound of timber on timber; danger; skill; uncertainty; the fall of the mighty; the triumph of the humble.

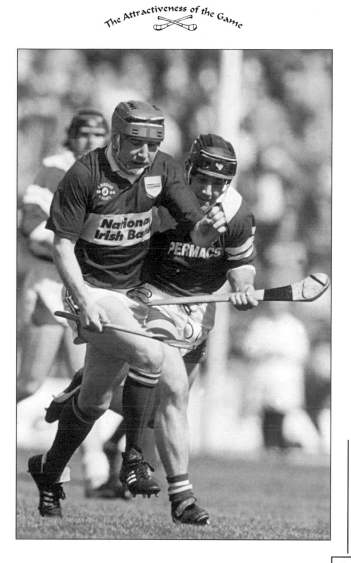

For the duration of a game the crowd is held spellbound in a state of suspended animation. They love scores. And these can come from any angle and from distances of ninety yards — even one hundred yards. They watch ordinary men doing extraordinary deeds — deeds of valour, known in Irish as *gaiscí* — blocking, hooking, batting, kicking, hand-passing, shoulder-to-shoulder physical challenges.

Games produce heroes. They give us the successors to Cú Chulainn — Giants and Legends, the stuff of myth, yet flesh and blood.

> *Camáin á luascadh ar fud na páirce*
> *Is an sliotar ag imeacht ar luas in airde.*
> Hurleys swinging throughout the field
> And the sliotar soaring at speed on high

Chapter Six

The Diaspora

Sé mo chas a bheith míle míle i gcéin
Ó bhán-chnoic Éireann Ó.
It is my plight to be many, many miles away
From the old fair hills of Ireland.

For Irish emigrants everywhere the game of hurling was, and still is, a link with the Homeland. It is also an expression of Irishness — a unique pastime that confers a badge of identity.

In every decade since the GAA was founded, countless hurling men have emigrated. Some returned after a while; others made occasional trips home; many, however, lived out their lives and were buried in 'Far Foreign Fields', *i bhfad ó bhaile.*

On 16 September 1888, forty-eight Irish athletes — among them hurlers — sailed for the United States on board the *Wisconsin*. They received a most enthusiastic reception when they arrived in New York. Throughout the trip, which has become known as 'The American Invasion', they participated in hurling exhibitions and athletic contests. A downside to the venture was the fact that seventeen of those who travelled remained in the States — among them John S. Mitchell of

Emly, a weight-thrower who made many world records during his career. Some others subsequently returned to reside permanently in the States. They included William Prendergast of Clonmel, Secretary of the Association 1888–89.

Mitchell started to write for the *New York Sun* and became a leading sporting journalist. Prendergast played a key role in securing the Celtic Park Grounds, New York, for Gaelic athletic fixtures.

A team of emigrants representing London won the All-Ireland hurling title of 1901 when they defeated Cork by 1:5 to 0:4.

In the Summer of 1911, a team of Irish-American hurlers, drawn from Chicago and New York and originally from the counties of Cork, Tipperary, Limerick, Offaly and Kilkenny, toured Ireland and played a series of matches that involved games at Wexford v Wexford, at Thurles v Tipperary, at Waterford v Kilkenny and at Jones's Road v Dublin.

The Tailteann Games of 1924, '28 and '32 afforded emigrants the opportunity to visit the Homeland. In 1928 the American team included Henry Meagher, brother of the renowned Lory of Kilkenny. Also on the team was Jack Keoghan who won an All-Ireland with Kilkenny when the final of 1907 was played at Dungarvan in the Summer of 1908.

Pat Leamy of Tipperary played on the American Tailteann games team of 1932. He was still playing in 1951 — aged 53 — when he manned the goal for New York in the National

League Final against Galway in New York. Egan Clancy, who starred with Limerick in the early years of the century, emigrated to Philadelphia where he played the game and wrote a GAA column in a leading American weekly.

Paddy McInerney, a native of Clare, who made his name in the green and white of Limerick, with All-Ireland wins in 1918 and 1921, went to the States in the 1920s. He died in New Mexico in 1983 — aged 88. In a photo he sent me in 1981 he was proudly holding the camán — 'as the saying goes I was born with a hurley in my hand'.

Steve Gallagher, brother of the great Josie of Galway fame, departed from our shores in the late 1940s to make a life for himself in the US where he continued his hurling career. Terry Leahy, hero of the 1947 All-Ireland Final, left his native Kilkenny for America before the end of that decade. He took with him his hurley. In the 'Land of the Free' he was known in hurling circles as Mr Hurling, and his deeds with the camán were magical.

Brendan Hennessy, at the age of 20, emigrated from Kerry to the US on 2 February 1958 — one of John B. Keane's 'Many Young Men of Twenty'. He was accompanied by five of the Ballyduff senior team. They had with them their hurleys. The game of hurling lessened their sense of exile, defined them, and was oxygen to their lives and the blood and bones of their existence. Brendan later recalled, 'Gaelic Park was number one meeting place for the Irish in New York. That's where the contacts were made for work and most of us met our wives there'.

The foregoing are but a few. The list is endless.

In May 1936 a great Limerick team set sail to tour the US. Dan Parker, an American commentator, writing in the *New York Daily Mirror*, had this to say about the game of hurling:

> *Nothing reflects the temperament of a people more accurately than the games they play. Hurling is Ireland's national pastime, and if you have never seen a hurling match I beg of you to defer awarding the palm to hockey, football, lacrosse or polo as a he-man's game until you have had Erin's game demonstrated to you by two good teams. Hurling combines the best features of baseball, a heavy-weight elimination tournament, hockey, a battle royal, golf and football.*
>
> *It is no game for a fellow with a dash of lavender in his makeup. A good hurler must be prepared at all times to stop, pick his head up from the field of battle, slap it back into position and resume the fray without once taking one eye off the player he's assigned to watch and the other off the enemy's goal. Having seen a hurling match one can understand readily why so many of the pioneers of baseball were of Irish blood, and why*

those of Celtic stock took naturally to America's game. Their encounters have been making one-hand catches and sharpening their battling eyes ever since Finn MacCool invented the game of hurling with an oak tree and a Dane's skull.

A good hurling team will keep the ball in the air longer than a juggler. It is permissible to catch it with one hand, usually the left, and as it comes sailing through the air, and give it a hearty belt with the end of the club. Clever hurlers can pass the ball from hurley to hurley as if they had lacrosse sticks. The teamwork is magnificent to behold. So is the mayhem. The first rule of hurling is to keep your eye on the ball and let your opponent's skull fall where it may. However, despite the terrific amount of shillelagh swinging there are surprisingly few serious casualties. The proverbial luck of the Irish seems to be with every hurler who dashes headlong at an opponent swinging his own club at the very same ball at which the opposing player is taking a pot shot.

It takes a strong physique to stand up under an hour of hurling, for the pace is swift as well as gruelling. It is little wonder that the Irish have no plagiarists in hurling. They invented the game, and though they haven't copyrighted it, no other race has attempted to play it. I suppose the explanation is that no other race is constituted temperamentally like the Irish. However, if it takes an Irishman to enjoy playing the game, one need not be a Celt to get a kick out of watching it. Anyone who watches a hurling game is both fascinated and amused by it. So to those who demand an exotic sports thrill I recommend a visit to a hurling match.

Seamus King, in his book *The Clash of the Ash in Foreign Fields* wrote in his Foreword:

> *Even before the foundation of the GAA hurling was played wherever Irishmen found themselves in the world. The game was played by the fishermen in Newfoundland, by Irish soldiers in the British Army in New York at the time of the American revolution and by the thousands of Wild Geese who manned the Battalions of the Irish Brigade on the continent of Europe.*

The game was also played — but only by the Irish — in Canada, Australia and even Argentina.

In 1934, the Jubilee Year of the GAA, the annual congress was held in Thurles on 1 April. At it, messages were read from Gaels in America, Britain, the Argentine, Australia and South Africa.

Brother T.N. O'Brien, a Christian Brother based in Buenos Aires, Argentina, tells the following story:

> *We used play a bit of hurling here on the beach during holiday, just pucking about. People would stop to watch us for a while. On one occasion an elderly gentleman asked me what game we were playing. I didn't feel like giving a long description of hurling so I asked if he had seen an exceptionally good hockey match. He told me he had seen the very best. 'Then,' I said, 'you know now what bad hurling is.'*

The Gaels beyond the Wave
(Air: 'The Dawning of the Day')

Whilst love and praise we e'er accord
The men of might and brawn,
Who foot the leather o'er the sward,
And wield the stout camán:
We'll not forget the exiled ones,
Our brothers stout and brave,
Who plod and toil on foreign soil —
The Gaels beyond the wave!

In English fields and mills and mines,
You'll find our young men there,
And where the burning sunlight shines,
On Pampas broad and fair;
And 'mid the deep Canadian woods,
And where the wild beasts rave,
In every sphere, where'er you steer —
The Gaels beyond the wave!

Amongst the cities famed and fair
Of Europe, they'll be found:
Some hold the highest honours there,
Some tread the cloistered ground;
And down by where the Tiber sweeps,
Where lies our princes' grave,
They are loyal and true, and not a few —
The Gaels beyond the wave!

Upon the barren African veld
You'll find our lads today,
And in Australia, too, the Celt
Has nobly won his way;
And 'neath the friendly 'Stars and Stripes',
That oft they died to save;
They are here and there and everywhere —
The Gaels beyond the wave!

Phil O'Neill 'Sliabh Ruadh'

Chapter Seven

Cultural and Social

With the exception of Antrim who, over the decades, made great efforts to promote the game, and, to a lesser extent, Down and Derry in modern times, the strongholds of hurling are to be found south of a line drawn on the map from Galway to Dublin. In that geographical area, the five counties have won national league titles and All-Ireland titles in all grades of hurling. They are Cork, Tipperary, Limerick, Wexford and Kilkenny.

The game knits a community together. It becomes part of the social fabric. It generates debate and conversation. Victory creates a glow of pride. Everyone basks in the reflected glory of success. Nothing illustrates this better than the 1944 Munster Final between Cork and Limerick. Sean Kilfeather in his publication, *Vintage Carbery*, gave this vivid account:

> One missed the long ranges of petrol-driven cars from the spacious square of Dr Croke. One missed them on the highroad and was glad of their absence on the byways. One missed, too, the thousands of eager enthusiasts from the cities that flowed out of Thurles Railway Station from the special trains in the

days that are gone — days that will come again, and the sooner the better! Yet it was always a gallant and typical Thurles final day. All the brightness and good cheer of the hospitable Cathedral town were there. Hundreds of well-known faces, hero-hurlers of past decades and generations. On the roads from Cork, Limerick and Kilkenny perspiring cyclists were plugging their way in. From the top of a low hill outside Thurles town I saw them coming in happy droves along the straight roads like ants on the move. Big Jim Hurley had cycled all the way from Cork and stayed overnight threshing out hurling history with the famous Leahy family of Boherlahan. Too bad I missed that seanacaidheacht on the eve of the final!

And such a final! A final that had a heart-throbbing pulsating finish that took people's breath away, and yet was no final at all; for these sparkling hurlers live to fight another day — July 30th, at the same ideal venue steeped in hurling history. Rural Ireland looked well on the way there and back — a day of soft, fleecy clouds that lent light and shade and colour to the mid-summer hills — a faint sprinkle of rain to lay the dust; the Galtees a study in blues and emeralds rising nobly over the fertile Golden Vein. Grass-lands not so luxuriant as usual; corn and potatoes doing fine; beet and other roots recovering slowly from the drought; hay well saved in fair measure of yield. An air of peace and comfort over all.

Pleasant it was meeting the genial priests, always associated with hurling finals in Thurles: Fr Hamilton of Clare, Fathers Lee, Fogarty and Meagher of Thurles, Fr Punch of Limerick; the GAA chiefs led in his Grace, Archbishop Kinnane, of the See of Cashel and Emly — typical athletic son of Tipperary. Many All-Ireland Captains living in the past: Willie Gleeson of Fedamore, Tim Gleeson of Drumbane, Denis Barry Murphy, Pat Collins, Liam Walsh of Cork, Denis Lanigan, Jim Humphries of the great Limerick sides, John Joe Sheehy, the Kerry star; Christy Leehy of Aherlow Glen; Chris Ryan of Mitchelstown; John Rochford of Kilkenny, who is the holder of seven All-Ireland medals; Jim (Hawk) O'Brien of Thurles, Hugh Shelly, James Maher and John Joe Callanan, the peerless forward; Phil Purcell, John Joe Hayes — hurlers champion hurlers all!

The game was beautifully controlled, the pitch a picture and the hurling hearty clean and fair.

I thought the first half somewhat subdued. Good sweet hitting on both sides; close marking, polished movement of swinging ash, fit, well-matched men. We had to wait for the second half for the fireworks, the heavy thud of crashing body to body and splintering ash — winding up in a crescendo of excitement. 'Was it the best second half ever?' people asked me after the game. I was silent; I could only smile inwardly; it was good and very good, dramatic and a wondrous sporting finish, fit to take its place among the greatest of out-door sporting spectacles that any land can boast! And memory tracked back to many such finals on this same pitch, perhaps more long-sustained and gripping yet never one that more completely gladdened the hurler's heart. We don't love drawn games, yet here was one that left no doubting Thomases — it was a truly played and glorious finish carrying all the fire and brilliancy of the great Munster hurling finals of the past.

They broke at lightning pace, and Archbishop Kinnane, who threw the ball in, was scarcely on the sideline when Cork raced in and Quirke placed Morrison, a tall bony youth —

smacked a grand ball past Walsh — Cork one goal up.
Breasting the ball well, Cottrell and Donovan sent Cork away
again and John Quirke's eye was dead in — he pulled on a hard
ground ball that gave Mickie Walsh no chance at all. Limerick
woke up and Tim Ryan hit a lovely ball that reached Mick
Mackey. That veteran player trapped it well and doubled carefully to the net for Limerick's opening goal. Cork forwards
again sparkled. Kelly and Ring were moving fast and once
more John Quirke's experience told — he dummied fast and
pulled hard and low — net. Cork two goals clear and going
well. Mulcahy next shone in beating back a Limerick bom-
bardment. John Power was holding John Lynch well. Then
young McCarthy, a tall rangy boy, landed a perfect point
for Limerick from a free. Clohessy and Stokes raised sailing
points but Cork were again two goals clear when Sean Condon
pointed a beauty score. Cork 3-1; Limerick 1-3.

Cottrell lifted and slipped through to hit a great point from
the 50 line but M. Mackey was back and hit a perfect point from
a fast moving ground pass. Cork were again away and a regular
storm of men swept in on Walsh before he was bundled into the
net — Cork's fourth goal. Stokes was deadly accurate with a free
for Limerick but they were seven points behind at half-way —
4-3 to 1-5 and the game looked all over for Cork with the wind,
sun and way to aid. Christy Ring and Stokes exchanged minor
scores and delightful hurling. Mick Mackey had another, but that
speedy Farranferris youth, Kelly, sprinted past and drove home,
Cork's fifth goal — John Lynch's free set the score 19 to 11 —
Limerick fighting hard against heavy odds.

Again these green jerseyed boys stormed in on Mulcahy and
Thornhill's lines. John Power, Tim Ryan and McCarthy were

rising to a great occasion. Power hit a long one — Dick Stokes trapped it and raced clear before letting fly for a smashing goal that set the crowd roaring. Kelly had another lovely point, but Stokes' goal had electrified Limerick. They moved like mowers in a meadow. Mackey was in his element now and when he dodged through and whipped a goal home, hats, coats, umbrellas and all went sky high — Score 21-19. Kelly and Stokes swapped points in a scintillating finish. Clohessy fastened on one and crashed it home for Limerick's lead, and pandemonium outside the lines — 20,000 swaying.

John Mackey set the score 24-22 in Limerick's favour. Broken time now. Then came John Quirke's greatest goal of his long career. Ring swung a pass to the old Rockie, Lynch helped to guard him. Quirke dummied twice and then shot. He knew a goal was the only rescue — he hit a beauty dead on the net for a goal and Cork's lead. Dead on time Stokes, cool as cold steel, landed above the bar for the balancing score — 25 all. And they meet again!

I wasn't in Thurles in 1944 — too young — but I was in Croke Park over fifty years later for the 1995 Leinster Final between Offaly and Kilkenny — a game I wrote about in *Legends of the Ash*:

What an absorbing contest we witnessed in 1995. Best game of the year it was — hurling in all its grandeur, where ash was swung with freedom and abandon in sporting, manly spirit. It was as if the gods knew what was in store and sent the elements to oblige us with a stirring prologue just as Kilkenny took the field: thunder, lightning, torrential rain, fans in the new Cusack Stand scattering and scurrying for cover. Right from the throw-in it was eyeball-to-eyeball stuff. No quarter anywhere on the pitch. Every score would be hard-earned: sweat and toil; sweat and toil. Offaly pressure was sustained and unrelenting. Every man had a task; the sum of all the tasks was a game plan — a team effort. Co-ordination, concentration, no panic, grim resolve — it all produced a synergy that slowly and gradually wore down the Kilkenny resistance. At half time it was five points to three points — low scoring but breathtaking and energy-sapping stuff. We marvelled at the splendour of the hurling — splendid and absorbing despite the atrocious weather.

The first score and the first goal could be crucial in the second half — and so it proved. Both came to Offaly in the second and seventh minutes. The goal, a probing outfield shot from Dáithí Regan, was a little fortuitous — but fortune favours the brave. Onward Offaly surged, their grip on the game growing more vice-like as the second half progressed. Between the tenth and eighteenth minute they were scoring at the rate of one point a minute and, as 'Carbery' would have said, 'moving like mowers in a meadow', Kilkenny probed and prodded; they contested and counter-attacked. But the Offaly defence was phalanx-like, blocking, hooking, parrying, harassing, droppucking, covering, batting, chasing. No way through.

About the twenty-seventh minute Pat O'Connor scored a smashing Offaly goal. He won the pull as he doubled on an overhead dropping ball on the edge of the square. The scoreboard read 2:14 to 0:5, and it was still that way with five minutes to go. Spectators blinked in disbelief.

For about three-quarters of the game Kevin Kinahan had been magnificent on D.J. Carey, and then D.J. moved outfield. In the last five minutes two flashes of D.J. genius brought two consolation goals, and the final score read Offaly 2:16, Kilkenny 2:5.

Éamon Cregan must have felt very proud of his Offaly team. He had seen his hurling philosophy translated into visible action by a dedicated and disciplined group of hurlers who responded to his promptings and gave us a performance that matched all the epics we had heard and read about from bygone years. It was entertainment at its best from the aristocrats of modern hurling — aristocrats who specialise in playing vintage hurling when they face Kilkenny. We had witnessed a Homeric contest — compliments of Offaly and Kilkenny. The spellbound Yank was right when he exclaimed, having witnessed a game in the thirties: 'It's a game for the gods.'

The Postal Authorities recognised the role of hurling in the sporting life of the nation and the contribution it made to society. In 1934, the jubilee year of the GAA, a stamp depicting a hurler was issued. Again in 1984, the centenary year of the GAA, the game was similarly commemorated.

Christy Ring, one of hurling's legends, has a monument erected to his memory in his native Cloyne, and in Cork City a bridge is named after him. In Annacotty, County Limerick, a life-size, action study monument in bronze commemorates Jackie Power, another legendary hurler (see page 76).

Hurling, like Gaelic football, proved to be a great healer after the Civil War of the early 1920s. It healed wounds that might otherwise have festered.

The magnetism of the game has attracted people from all walks of life and disparate backgrounds — 'the butcher, the baker, the candlestick maker'. And for that one hour on the hurling pitch all are 'equal made'.

One of those drawn to the game became Taoiseach (Prime Minister) of Ireland from 1966 to 1973 and again from 1977 to 1979. He was Jack Lynch of Cork, winner of six All-Ireland senior medals in a row, 1941–1946 inclusive (football in 1945). According to Jack:

> I think that hurling typifies the Irish character and tradition more than anything else, with the exception of our language. It has a combination of skill, courage, speed of thought and action, and calls for a spirit of give and take more than most games. Its main implement is a stick skilfully hewn and fashioned from the ash tree, which grows so abundantly in our land. Can anything be more racy of the soil — the game itself, the camán, the men who play it?

Chapter Eight

Competitions and Grades

Nowadays, several grades of competition exist in hurling. But that wasn't always the case. After the foundation of the GAA in 1884 only one grade existed — the senior championship. And this was the position for the first twenty-five years of the GAA.

In 1912 the junior grade was introduced, and Cork were the first to win the title.

With a view to further promoting and fostering the game among the youth the minor grade was established in 1928. Those eligible to participate had to be under 18 years of age on 1 January in the year of each championship. Cork captured the first title.

The age limit wasn't always observed in the early days. There were cases of blatant disregard — so much so that consideration was given at one stage in the 1930s to abandoning the competition. But good sense prevailed — those in authority ensured that the age limit was strictly observed and the competition went from success to success. Games in that category, with many players having school and college experience, have produced superb exhibitions of hurling.

So popular was the game becoming that a National League for senior teams was initiated in 1925–26. Cork confirmed their status in the hurling world by winning the first title. The Limerick team of the 1930s really glamorised the competition and won five titles in a row from 1934 to 1938 — a record that still stands.

The Railway Cup competition came into being in 1927. This was an inter-provincial competition. The final took place on St Patrick's Day at Croke Park. The first final between Munster and Leinster produced a delightful exhibition of the ancient game, with victory going to Leinster by a margin of two points. The competition grew in popularity and for the succeeding four decades attracted huge attendances to Croke Park. Unfortunately, its status as a crowd-drawing competition went into decline in the 1970s. Efforts have been made in recent times to revitalise it by playing the games at provincial venues.

In 1961 an intermediate grade was introduced. This catered for a standard between senior and junior. Wexford became the first title holders. The competition lapsed in 1974 but was revived again in 1998 when Limerick took the title — their first.

The jump from minor to senior grade was recognised as being in general too great for many minor players. Accordingly, with a view to bridging the gap, an under-21 competition was inaugurated in 1964. Tipperary were the first winners and the competition itself has continued to be an out-standing success ever since.

With the aim of strengthening, improving and consolidating the game in the lesser strongholds, a senior 'B' championship was introduced in 1974. Success in the competition provided a welcome boost for those who contributed so much towards the promotion and well-being of the game.

Chapter Nine

Founders of the GAA

Three names in particular are associated with the foundation of the GAA: Michael Cusack, Maurice Davin and Archbishop Croke.

Michael Cusack, a teacher by profession, was a native of County Clare — born and reared in the parish of Carron, in the barony of the Burren. He was the first Secretary of the GAA and held that position in the period 1884–85. 'Bring back the hurling!' was his clarion cry. Cusack died on 27 November 1906, aged 59.

Maurice Davin was an outstanding athlete — a world champion at the hammer-throw and 56lb weight. He was born in Deerpark, Carrick-on-Suir, County Tipperary. Warm-hearted and sincere, his strong principles and sense of justice, coupled with a cool and calm disposition, enabled him to make a major contribution to the GAA in its infancy. He was the GAA's first President, holding the position from 1884 to 1887. A dispute saw him resign his post but he was back again for a second term in 1888–89. He died in January 1927 in his eighty-fourth year, at his home in Deerpark.

Dr Thomas W. Croke, later to become Archbishop of Cashel, was born in Mallow, County Cork, in 1824. He was among the first patrons of the GAA. He believed deeply in its ideals and aspirations and was a staunch supporter of the movement until the time of his death in July 1902. His wisdom and negotiating skills solved many a problem in the early days of the Association.

Chapter Ten

The Greats

Great exponents of the game of hurling have graced the playing fields of Ireland in every decade since the foundation of the GAA. To pick a great fifteen is easy — for the simple reason that you could pick several. To pick a best ever is an impossibility.

In 1984 a Team of the Century was selected by public acclaim. It contained fifteen great men. And yet, not one player was selected from the first forty years of the GAA! Forgotten heroes? The team was selected mainly from an era of about thirty years. And each position on the field could have been manned by many of equal ability — though perhaps different in style from the chosen one.

I have decided to give a selection of teams from a variety of sources. It goes without saying that they merely scratch the surface as regards great ones.

P.D. Mehigan's team chosen in the mid 1950s — Carbery

John 'Skinny' O'Meara
(Tipperary)

Dan Coughlan   **Sean Óg Hanley**   **Mick Derivan**
(Cork)   **(Limerick)**   **(Galway)**

Pat Stakelum   **James Kelliher**   **Dick Grace**
(Tipperary)   **(Cork)**   **(Kilkenny)**

Lory Meagher   **Jim Hurley**
(Kilkenny)   **(Cork)**

Eugene Coughlan   **Mick Mackey**   **Tom Semple**
(Cork)   **(Limerick)**   **(Tipperary)**

Mattie Power   **Martin Kennedy**   **Christy Ring**
(Kilkenny)   **(Tipperary)**   **(Cork)**

The Greats

Tommy Doyle's team — star Tipperary hurler 1937–1953

Tony Reddin
(Tipperary)

Johnny Leahy   Sean Óg Murphy   John Joe Doyle
(Tipperary)   (Cork)   (Clare)

John Keane   Paddy Clohessy   Paddy Phelan
(Waterford)   (Limerick)   (Kilkenny)

Jim Hurley   Lory Meagher
(Cork)   (Kilkenny)

Christy Ring   Mick Mackey   Phil Cahill
(Cork)   (Limerick)   (Tipperary)

Eudi Coughlan   Martin Kennedy   Mattie Power
(Cork)   (Tipperary)   (Kilkenny)

Jack Lynch's team — star Cork hurler and footballer 1935–1951

Paddy Scanlon
(Limerick)

Paddy Larkin	**Nick O'Donnell**	**Willie Murphy**
(Kilkenny)	**(Wexford)**	**(Cork)**

Tommy Doyle	**John Keane**	**Billy Rackard**
(Tipperary)	**(Waterford)**	**(Wexford)**

Eudi Coughlan   **Timmy Ryan**
(Cork)   **(Limerick)**

Christy Ring	**Mick Mackey**	**Jimmy Langton**
(Cork)	**(Limerick)**	**(Kilkenny)**

Eddie Keher	**Nicky Rackard**	**Josie Gallagher**
(Kilkenny)	**(Wexford)**	**(Galway)**

Phil Shanahan's team — star Tipperary midfielder 1948–1957

'Skinny' O'Meara
(Tipperary)

John Keane   Bobby Rackard   John Joe Doyle
(Waterford)   (Wexford)   (Clare)

Tommy Doyle   Tony Wall   Jimmy Finn
(Tipperary)   (Tipperary)   (Tipperary)

Timmy Ryan   Phil Shanahan
(Limerick)   (Tipperary)

Christy Ring   Mick Mackey   Jimmy Doyle
(Cork)   (Limerick)   (Tipperary)

Eddie Keher   Martin Kennedy   Jackie Power
(Kilkenny)   (Tipperary)   (Limerick)

Paddy Quirke's team — a brilliant Carlow hurler 1974–1990

Noel Skehan
(Kilkenny)

Aidan Fogarty   Pat Hartigan   John Horgan
(Offaly)   (Limerick)   (Cork)

Mick Jacob   Ger Henderson   Iggy Clarke
(Wexford)   (Kilkenny)   (Galway)

Frank Cummins   Paddy Quirke
(Kilkenny)   (Carlow)

Johnny Callinan   Martin Quigley   John Fenton
(Clare)   (Wexford)   (Cork)

Eamon Cregan   Tony Doran   Eddie Keher
(Limerick)   (Wexford)   (Kilkenny)

Aidan Fogarty's team — a stalwart Offaly defender 1976–1991

Noel Skehan
(Kilkenny)

Joe Hennessy   **Leonard Enright**   **Sylvie Linnane**
(Kilkenny)   (Limerick)   (Galway)

Aidan Fogarty   **Ger Henderson**   **John Taylor**
(Offaly)   (Kilkenny)   (Laois)

Frank Cummins   **Joe Cooney**
(Kilkenny)   (Galway)

Billy Fitzpatrick   **Martin Quigley**   **P.J. Molloy**
(Kilkenny)   (Wexford)   (Galway)

Pat Fox   **Joe McKenna**   **Liam Fennelly**
(Tipperary)   (Limerick)   (Kilkenny)

Tony Doran's team —legendary Wexford full forward 1967–1984

(In the words of Con Houlihan 'The Happy Warrior')

Noel Skehan
(Kilkenny)

Fan Larkin   **Pat Hartigan**   **Dan Quigley**
(Kilkenny)   (Limerick)   (Wexford)

Ger Henderson   **Mick Roche**   **Iggy Clarke**
(Kilkenny)   (Tipperary)   (Galway)

Phil Wilson   **Frank Cummins**
(Wexford)   (Kilkenny)

Jimmy Doyle   **Pat Delaney**   **Eddie Keher**
(Tipperary)   (Kilkenny)   (Kilkenny)

Ray Cummins   **Tony Doran**   **Eamon Cregan**
(Cork)   (Wexford)   (Limerick)

The Greats

Willie Barron's team — brilliant Waterford half forward 1937–1946

Tony Reddin
(Tipperary)

Willie Murphy   Nick O'Donnell   Andy Fleming
(Cork)   (Wexford)   (Waterford)

Dick Stokes   John Keane   Jackie Power
(Limerick)   (Waterford)   (Limerick)

Jack Lynch   Christy Moylan
(Cork)   (Waterford)

Willie Barron   Mick Mackey   Jimmy Doyle
(Waterford)   (Limerick)   (Tipperary)

Christy Ring   Joe McKenna   Johnny Quirke
(Cork)   (Limerick)   (Cork)

'Sambo' McNaughton's team — brilliant Antrim hurler 1980–1997

Ger Cunningham
(Cork)

Sylvie Linnane   Brian Lohan   Brian Corcoran
(Galway)   (Clare)   (Cork)

Peter Finnerty   Ger Henderson   Brian Whelehan
(Galway)   (Kilkenny)   (Offaly)

Ciaran Carey   John Fenton
(Limerick)   (Cork)

Martin Storey   Michael Coleman   D.J. Carey
(Wexford)   (Galway)   (Kilkenny)

Pat Fox   Joe Cooney   Nicky English
(Tipperary)   (Galway)   (Tipperary)

CHRISTY RING

Camogie

The game of hurling is also played by women, when it is called Camogie. It was officially established in 1904 and progressed slowly from there.

Teams consist of twelve aside. The rules are similar to those of hurling, but the pitch is shorter and narrower. The emphasis is on strictly playing the ball at all times. Aggressive physical contact is prohibited.

In 1932 the first senior All-Ireland camogie championship took place and Dublin won the title — beating Galway in the final. Down the decades, the leading powers in the game have been Dublin, Cork, Kilkenny, Antrim, Wexford and, to a lesser extent, Galway, Tipperary and Limerick.

The game has had its legends and superstars. Pride of place must go to the late Kathleen Mills of Dublin who, in a career that stretched from 1942 to 1961, won fifteen All-Ireland medals. She is followed by fellow county colleague, Una O'Connor, who won thirteen All-Ireland medals between 1953 and 1966.

Without a doubt, the Cú Chulainn of modern day camogie has been Angela Downey of Kilkenny. Immensely talented and versatile, she has given many scintillating performances in a career that saw her win twelve All-Ireland medals. Her twin sister Ann, not far behind Angela in ability, also won twelve All-Ireland medals. Their father, Shem, won an All-Ireland senior hurling title with Kilkenny in the 1947 classic final with Cork.

Other camogie heroines include Mary O'Leary and Marian McCarthy of Cork, Eithne Leech and Orla Ní Shíocháin of Dublin, Liz Neary of Kilkenny, Margaret O'Leary-Lacey of Wexford and Máiréad McAtamney-Magill of Antrim.

Table of Success

ULSTER — MUNSTER CONNAUGHT

County	Senior	Junior **	Minor	Inter-mediate	Under 21	N.L.	Senior B	Total
Antrim	-	-	-	1	-	-	3	4
Derry	-	-	-	-	-	-	1	1
Down	-	1	-	-	-	-	-	1
Monaghan	-	1	-	-	-	-	-	1
Clare	3	2	1	-	-	3	-	9
Cork	27	11	17	1	11	14	-	81
Kerry	1	2	-	-	-	-	3	6
Limerick	7	4	3	1	1	11	-	27
Tipperary	24	9	16	4	8	16	-	77
Waterford	2	2	2	-	1	1	-	8
Galway	4	2	3	-	7	6	-	22
Roscommon	-	1	-	-	-	-	1	2

** *The status of this competition has altered from time to time with a view to accomodating the weaker counties.*

Table of Success

 LEINSTER AND ENGLAND

County	Senior	Junior **	Minor	Inter-mediate	Under 21	N.L.	Senior B	Total
Carlow	-	-	-	1	-	-	1	2
Dublin	6	3	4	-	-	2	-	15
Kildare	-	2	-	1	-	-	3	6
Kilkenny	25	9	16	1	6	9	-	66
Laois	1	-	-	-	-	-	2	3
Meath	-	4	-	-	-	-	1	5
Offaly	4	2	3	-	-	1	-	10
Westmeath	-	1	-	-	-	-	3	4
Wexford	6	2	3	2	1	4	-	18
Wicklow	-	2	-	-	-	-	-	2
London	1	5	-	2	-	-	5	13
Warwick-shire	-	3	-	-	-	-		3

** *The status of this competition has altered from time to time with a view to accomodating the weaker counties.*

The Hurler's Prayer

Grant me, O Lord, a hurler's skill,

With strength of arm and speed of limb,

Unerring eye for the flying ball,

And courage to match whate'er befall.

May my stroke be steady and my aim be true,

My actions manly and my misses few;

No matter what way the game may go,

May I rest in friendship with every foe.

When the final whistle for me has blown,

And I stand at last before God's judgment throne,

May the Great Referee when He calls my name

Say, You hurled like a man; you played the game.

Seamus Redmond

Rules of Hurling

The following pages are reproduced from
The Rules of Hurling published by the Central Council
of the GAA. They are published courtesy of the GAA
who retain the copyright.

The Rules of Hurling

Rules of Fair Play

RULE 1 — THE PLAY

1.1 The ball is in play once it has been thrown in or pucked after the referee has given a signal to start or restart play, and it remains in play until:

(a) the referee signals a stop;

(b) the ball has passed completely over any boundary line or strikes any flag marking the boundary lines;

(c) the ball has been prevented from going over any boundary line or is touched in play by anyone other than a player.

1.2 The ball may be struck with the hurley when it is on the ground, in the air tossed from the hand or lifted with the hurley

1.3 A player may run with the ball balanced on, or hopping on his hurley.

1.4 A player may catch the ball, play it on his hurley and bring it back onto his hand once
A player who has not caught the ball may play it from the hurley into his hand twice.

1.5 The ball may be struck with the hand, kicked, or lifted off the ground with the feet

1.6 The ball may not be touched on the ground with the hand(s) except when a player is knocked down or falls, and the ball in his hand touches the ground.

1.7 The ball may be carried in the hand for a maximum of four consecutive steps or held in the hand for no longer than the time needed to take four steps.

1.8 Player(s) may tackle an opponent for the ball.

1.9 Provided that he has at least one foot on the ground, a player may make a side-to-side charge on an opponent:-

(a) who is in possession of the ball, or

(b) who is playing the ball, or

(c) when both players are moving in the direction of the ball to play it.

When he is within the small rectangle, the goalkeeper may not be charged but he may be challenged for possession of the ball and his puck, kick or pass may be blocked. Incidental contact with the goalkeeper while playing the ball is permitted.

1.10 For a run-up to a free puck, side-line puck, or puck-out, a player may go outside the boundary lines, but otherwise players shall remain within the field of play.

1.11 A player may hold up his hurley or hand(s) to intercept a free puck

RULE 2 - SET PLAY

2.1 The referee, facing the players, starts the game and re-starts it after half-time by throwing in the ball between two players from each team, whc shall stand one behind the other in their own defensive sides of the half-way line. All other players shall be in their respective positions behind the 65m lines.

2.2 After a foul, play is restarted by a free puck or a throw-in where the foul(s) occurred.

EXCEPTIONS

(i) In the case of fouls by defending players within the rectangles, the following shall apply:

A penalty puck shall be awarded for an Aggressive Foul within the large rectangle. The penalty puck shall be taken from the centre point of the 20m line. A free puck shall be awarded for a Technical Foul within the large rectangle.

(ii) A free puck awarded for a foul by a defending player inside his own 20m line but outside the large rectangle shall be taken from the 20m line opposite where the foul occurred.

(iii) When a player is fouled immediately after he plays the ball away, and a score results, it shall stand. Otherwise, the referee shall award a free-puck from where the foul occurred or, if more

advantageous, from where the ball lands or crosses the side-line. With the option of a free being awarded from where the foul occurred being retained, the rule shall apply in the following circumstances:-

(a) If the ball lands over the end-line, a free shall be given on the 20m line opposite the place where the ball crossed the end-line.

(b) If the ball lands inside the opponents' 20m line, a free shall be given from the 20m line opposite the place where the ball crossed this line.

(iv) Where otherwise specified in the penalties listed in Rule 4, Sections 14, 15, 16, 17, 18, 19, 28, 29, 30 31 and Rule 6.2

(v) When play is re-started by throwing in the ball after a foul(s) between the end-line and the 20m line, the throw-in shall be given on the 20m line, opposite where the foul(s) occurred.

All players except the player taking the free puck (excluding penalties), shall be 20m from where the free puck is being taken or all players except those two contesting the throw-in shall be 13m from where the throw-in is awarded.

2.3 A penalty puck shall be taken at the centre point of the 20m line and the semi-circular arc and only three defending players may stand on the goal-line. All other players, with the exception of the player taking the puck, shall be outside the 20m line, and shall not cross the 20m line or the arc until the ball has been struck. If a defending player(s) fouls before the ball is struck and a goal does not result, the referee shall allow the penalty puck to be retaken.

2.4   When opposing players foul simultaneously, play is restarted by throwing in the ball.

2.5   For all free pucks, including penalties, the ball may be struck with the hurley in either of two ways:

(a) Lift the ball with the hurley at the first attempt and strike it with the hurley.

(b) Strike the ball on the ground.

If a player taking a free puck or penalty fails to lift the ball at the first attempt, or fails to strike it away with the hurley, he must strike it on the ground without delay. Only when he delays, may a player of either side approach nearer than 20m except in the case of penalties.

2.6   When the ball is played over the end-line by the team attacking that end or after a score, play is restarted by a puck-out from within the small rectangle.

The player taking a puck-out shall take the ball into his hand, but should he miss his stroke, the ball may be struck on the ground or may be raised with and struck with the hurley, but not taken into his hand again before striking it. The player taking the puck-out may strike the ball more than once before another player touches it.

All players shall be outside the 20m line until the ball has been struck except the goalkeeper

and the player taking the puck-out - if other than the goalkeeper.

The ball shall travel 13m before being played by another player of the defending team.

2.7   When the ball is played over the end-line and outside the goal-posts by the team defending that end, a free puck shall be awarded to the opposing team on the 65m line opposite where the ball crossed the end-line.

2.8   When the team plays the ball over the side-line, a free puck from the ground shall be awarded to the opposing team at the place where the ball crossed the side-line. If opposing players play the ball simultaneously over the side-line, or if the officials are not sure which team played the ball last, the linesman shall throw in the ball between one player from each team. A ball that strikes a side-line or corner flag shall be treated as having crossed the side-line. A player on the team awarded a side-line puck shall place the ball on the side-line at the place indicated by the linesman. All players except the player taking the side-line puck, or the two players contesting the throw-in, shall be at least 13m from the ball until it is struck or thrown in.

If a player taking a side-line puck fails to strike the ball at the first attempt, he shall not delay in making a second attempt. Only when the player delays his second attempt to strike the

ball may a player from either side approach
nearer than 13 m.

2.9 If the ball touches any non-player during play,
play is restarted by throwing in the ball at the
place concerned, but if the ball touches any
non-player from a free puck, the free shall be
retaken.

EXCEPTIONS

(i) As provided in Rule 3.3(a).

(ii) If the ball has been prevented from going
over a boundary line by a non-player
other than the referee, it shall be treated
as having crossed the line and the
referee shall make the appropriate
award.

RULE 3 — SCORES

3.1 A **goal** is scored when the ball is played over
the goal line between the posts and under the
crossbar by either team.

A **point** is scored when the ball is played over
the crossbar between the posts by either team.
A goal is equivalent to three points.
The team with the greater final total of points is
the winner.

EXCEPTIONS

A player on the team attacking a goal and who
is in possession of the ball may not score;

(i) by carrying the ball over his opponents'
goal-line, or

(ii) with his hand(s).

3.2 A score may be made by striking the ball in
flight with the hand(s).

3.3 (a) A score shall be allowed if, in the opinion of the
referee, the ball was prevented from crossing
the goal-line by anyone other than a player or
the referee.

(b) If part of the goal-posts or crossbar is
displaced during play, the referee shall award
the score which he considers would have
resulted had a part not been displaced.

3.4 If a defending player plays the ball through his
own scoring space in any manner, this shall
count as a score.

Rules of Foul Play

RULE 4 — TECHNICAL FOULS

4.1 To overcarry or overhold the ball.

4.2 To throw the ball.

4.3 To lift the ball off the ground with the knees.

4.4 To lie on the ball.

4.5 To touch the ball on the ground with the hands except when a player falls or is knocked down and the ball in his hand touches the ground.

4.6 To catch the ball more than twice before playing it away.

4.7 To toss the ball with the hand and catch it without playing it with the hurley.

4.8 To drop the hurley intentionally or to throw the hurley in a manner which does not constitute a danger to another player.

4.9 To tip an opponent's hurley in the air or to tip it up with hurley or foot for the purpose of allowing the ball to pass through.

4.10 For an attacking player to enter opponents' small rectangle before the ball enters it during the play

EXCEPTIONS

(i) If an attacking player legally enters the small rectangle, and the ball is played from that area but is returned before the attacking player has time to leave the area, provided that he does not play the ball or interfere with the defence, a foul is not committed.

(ii) When a point is scored from outside the small rectangle and the ball is sufficiently high to be out of reach of all players, the score shall be allowed even though an attacking player may have been within the small rectangle before the ball - provided that the player in question does not interfere with the defence.

4.11 (a) For a player on the team awarded a free puck other than a penalty to stand or move nearer than 20m to the ball before it is struck.

(b) For a player on the team awarded a side-line puck to stand or move nearer than 13m to the ball before it is struck.

(c) For a player on the team awarded a penalty puck to be inside the 20m line or the arc before the ball is struck.

4.12 For a player attacking a goal to carry the ball over his opponents' goal-line.

4.13 For a player on the team attacking a goal, who is in possession of the ball, to score with the hand(s).

PENALTY FOR ABOVE FOULS - Free puck from where the foul occurred except as provided under EXCEPTIONS of Rule 2.2.

4.14 To be inside opponents' 20m line before a puck-out is taken after a wide.

PENALTY - Free puck from the defenders' 20m line opposite where the foul occurred.

4.15 To take the puck-out from outside the small rectangle.

PENALTY - 65m free puck opposite where the foul occurred.

4.16 (a) For a player on the team defending a penalty puck, with the exception of the three defending players on the goal-line, to be inside the 20m line or the semi-circle before the penalty puck is taken.

(b) For any of the three players defending a penalty on the goal-line to move nearer than 20m to the ball before the penalty puck is taken.

PENALTY - If a goal is not scored, the referee shall allow the penalty puck to be retaken.

4.17 (a) For an opposing player to be nearer than 20m to the ball before a free puck is struck.

(b) For an opposing player to be nearer than 13m to the ball before a side-line puck is struck.

PENALTY FOR THE ABOVE FOULS -

Free puck 13m more advantageous than the place of original puck - up to opponents' 20m line.

4.18 To delay an opponent taking a free puck or side-line puck by hitting or kicking the ball away, not

releasing the ball to the opposition, or by deliberately not moving back to allow the puck to be taken.

4.19 To interfere with a player taking a free puck or side-line puck by jumping up and down, waving hands or hurley or any other physical or verbal interference considered by the referee to be aimed at distracting the player taking the puck.

EXCEPTION

A player holding his hands or hurley upright shall not constitute an interference.

PENALTY - Free puck 13m more advantageous than the place of original puck - up to opponents' 20m line.

4.20 To reset the ball for a free / penalty / sideline puck without the referee's permission after the whistle has been blow for the free / penalty / sideline puck to be taken.

4.21 To play the ball again after taking a free / penalty / sideline puck before another player has played it, unless the ball rebounds off the goal-post(s) or crossbar.

4.22 To foul a free puck by making a second attempt to lift the ball, to hop the ball on the hurley, or to take the ball in the hand.

4.23 For the player taking a side-line puck to attempt to lift the ball with his hurley.

4.24 To make a divot for the purpose of teeing up the ball for a free puck or side-line puck.

4.25 To advance the ball deliberately from the place at which a free puck or side-line puck is to be taken.

4.26 To waste time by delaying a free puck or side-line puck awarded to own team.

PENALTY FOR THE ABOVE FOULS -
(i) Cancel free puck or side-line puck.
(ii) Throw in the ball where the foul occurred except as provided under EXCEPTION (v) of Rule 2.2.

4.27 For the player taking the puck-out and, having missed a stroke, to take the ball into his hand a second time before striking.

4.28 To be inside own 20m line when one's team is taking a puck-out except as provided in Rule 2.6.

4.29 For another player on the team taking the puck-out to play the ball before it has travelled 13m.

4.30 To waste time by delaying own puck-out.

PENALTY FOR ABOVE FOULS -
(i) Cancel puck-out.
(ii) Throw in the ball on defenders' 20m line opposite the scoring space.

4.31 For a player(s) from each team to foul simultaneously.

PENALTY - Throw in the ball where the foul(s) occurred except as provided under EXCEPTION (v) of Rule 2.2.

4.32 To go outside the boundary lines to gain an advantage except as permitted by Rule 1.10.

4.33 To interfere with the goal-posts to distract opponents or to gain an advantage.

PENALTY FOR THE ABOVE FOULS -
Caution offender; order off for second cautionable offence.

4.34 When a team commits a technical foul, the referee may allow the play to continue if he considers it to be to the advantage of the opposing team. Once he allows play to continue, he may not subsequently award a free for that foul. He shall apply any relevant disciplinary action.

RULE 5 — AGGRESSIVE FOULS

5.1 To strike or attempt to strike an opponent with a hurley, head, arm, elbow, hand or knee.

5.2 To kick or attempt to kick an opponent.

5.3 To stamp on an opponent.

5.4 To behave in any way which is dangerous to an opponent.

5.5 To strike, attempt to strike, to interfere with, to threaten, or to use abusive language or conduct to a match official.

PENALTY FOR THE ABOVE FOULS —
(i) Order offender off.
(ii) Free puck from where foul occurred except as provided under EXCEPTIONS of Rule 2.2.

5.6 To commit any of the fouls listed in Rule 5.1 to Rule 5.4 inclusive against a team-mate.

PENALTY —
(i) Order offender off.
(ii) Throw in the ball where the foul occurred except as provided under EXCEPTION (v) of Rule 2.2.

5.7 To commit any of the fouls listed in Rule 5.1 to Rule 5.4 inclusive on an opponent on the field prior to the start of the game or at half-time.

PENALTY . Offender shall be treated as ordered off and shall not participate (or further participate) in the game.

NOTE: Once the referee has received the list of players, or a substitution slip which includes the offender's name, the player may not be substituted.

5.8 To pull down an opponent

5.9 To trip an opponent with hand(s). foot, or hurley.

5.10 To jump at an opponent.

5.11 To threaten or to use abusive or provocative language or gestures to an opponent.

5.12 To engage in any form of rough play.

5.13 To make a 'pull' with the hurley from behind and around the body of an opponent that is not consistent with an attempt to play the ball.

5.14 To use the hurley in a careless manner.

5.15 To throw a hurley in a manner which constitutes a danger to another player(s).

5.16 To 'pull' with the hurley before the ball arrives.

PENALTY FOR ABOVE FOULS -
(i) Caution offender; order off for second cautionable foul.
(ii) Free puck from where the foul occurred except as provided under EXCEPTIONS of Rule 2.2.

5.17 To threaten or to use abusive or provocative language or gestures to a team-mate.

PENALTY FOR ABOVE FOULS —
(i) Caution offender; order off for second cautionable foul.
(ii) Throw in the ball where the foul occurred except as provided under EXCEPTION (v) of Rule 2.2.

5.18 (a) To push an opponent or hold an opponent with the hand(s) or hurley

(b) To hold opponent's hurley or pull it from his hand(s).

5.19 (a) To charge an opponent in the back or to the front.

(b) To charge an opponent unless
  (i) he is in possession of the ball, or
  (ii) he is playing the ball, or
  (iii) both players are moving in the direction of the ball to play it

(c) To charge an opponent for the purpose of giving an advantage to a team-mate.

(d) To charge the goalkeeper in his small rectangle

(e) For a player in possession of the ball to charge an opponent

5.20 To use the hurley to obstruct an opponent

5.21 To strike an opponent's hurley unless both players are in the act of striking the ball.

PENALTY FOR THE ABOVE FOULS —
(i) Free puck from where foul occurred except as provided under EXCEPTIONS of Rule 2.2
(ii) Caution offender for persistently committing such fouls; order off for second cautionable foul.

5.22 For a player to retaliate between the award of a free to his team and the free puck being taken.

PENALTY —
(i) Cancel free puck.
(ii) Throw in the ball where the original foul occurred except as provided under EXCEPTION (v) of Rule 2.2.
(iii) Apply any other relevant penalty of Rule 5.

5.23 For a player(s) from each team to foul simultaneously.

PENALTY —
(i) Throw in the ball where the fouls occurred except as provided under EXCEPTION (v) of Rule 2.2.
(ii) Apply any other relevant penalty of Rule 5.

5.24 When an Aggressive Foul is drawn to the referee's attention by an umpire or linesman, the referee may apply the appropriate penalty as per Rule 5 and shall restart play as per Rule 2.

5.25　When a team commits an Aggressive Foul, the referee may allow play to continue if he considers it to be to the advantage of the offended team. Once the referee allows the play to continue, he may not subsequently award a free for that foul. He shall apply the relevant penalty.

RULE 6 - DISSENT

6.1　To challenge the authority of a match official.

PENALTY - Caution the offender; order off for second cautionable foul.

6.2　To show dissent with the referee's decision to award a free puck to the opposing team.

PENALTY - The free puck already awarded shall be taken 13m more advantageous than the place of original free puck up to the opponents' 20m line.

6.3 (a)　To refuse to leave the field of play when ordered off.

(b)　To rejoin the game after being ordered off.

PROCEDURE
First give a three minute warning to the team captain or the official in charge of the team, or the player(s) involved, and then, if the player(s) refuse(s) to comply, terminate the game.

6.4　A team or a player(s) leaving the field without the referee's permission or refusing to continue playing.

PROCEDURE - as in Rule 6.3
Any player willing to continue shall give his name to the referee.

Important Terms and Definitions — Hurling and Football

The following list of Definitions of Terms used in the Playing Rules forms an integral part of these rules.

1. BOUNCE

For a player to play the ball against the ground with his hand(s) and back to his hand(s) again.

2. CATCH

To gain control of the ball with the hand(s) in a way which prevents it falling to the ground.

3. CAUTION

To take a player's name.

4. CHARGE (Fair)

Provided he has at least one foot on the ground, a player may make a side-to-side charge on an opponent (a) who is in possession of the ball, or (b) who is playing the ball, or (c) both players are moving in the direction of the ball to play it

5. DELAY (Deliberate)

Deliberately taking too much time to retrieve the ball, or to restart play, or any action which unduly delays the restart of play.

6. DIVOT

An elevation formed from the surface of the pitch for the purpose of teeing up the ball on the ground

7. HANDPASS

When in possession, the ball may be struck with the open hand or fist - provided there is a definite striking action, with the striking hand not being in contact with ball before delivering the strike.

In a two-handed pass, the ball may be struck off a holding hand by the other hand, or released and struck. In a one-handed pass, the ball shall be released from the hand before being struck by the same hand The releasing of the ball, when used, shall be considered an integral part of the hand fisted pass

8. FOUL

Aggressive

To physically or verbally abuse any player or official

Dissent

To disagree openly with any official about any decision

Technical

To foul the ball, or any other foul that is not aggressive or dissenting

9. IN FLIGHT — The ball is deemed to be in flight, once it is off the ground, having been played away within the Rules of Fair Play.

10. LIFT — To use the foot or feet to raise the ball from the ground to the hand(s).

11. OVERCARRY — To take more than four steps while holding the ball in the hand(s).

12. OVERHOLD — To hold the ball longer than is required to take four steps.

13. PLAY THE BALL — To touch the ball. The last player touching the ball before it crosses a boundary line shall be considered the last person playing it.

14. 'PULL' (FAIR) — To swing the hurley to play or attempt to play the ball.

15 TACKLE — Any attempt to dispossess or reduce the advantage of opponent within the Rules of Fair Play. With the exception of the charge (fair), the tackle is aimed at the ball not the player.

16. THROW — When the ball held in the hand(s) is played away without a definite striking action.

17. THROW-IN — To throw the ball up over the heads of one player from each team (football) or to throw the ball along the ground between one player from each team (hurling). For the start of the game and the restart after half-time, the throw-in shall be between two players from each team.

18. TOE-TAP — To release the ball from the hand(s) to the foot and kick it back into the hand(s).

19. TOSS (Football) — To release the ball from the hand(s) to kick it, toe-tap it, or pass it with the hand(s).

(Hurling) — To release the ball from the hand to strike it with the hurley, foot or hand.

20. WREST — To attempt to dispossess an opponent who already has a (firm) hold on the ball by grabbing the ball to take it from him.

THE WOLFHOUND GUIDE TO
THE SHAMROCK

Bob Curran

No other plant is as intertwined with both the history and folklore of Ireland as the shamrock. It has become the very symbol of Ireland and of Irishness world-wide. Like Ireland and her children, it has been extolled in song, story and poem.

In this fascinating book, Bob Curran explores the traditions of the shamrock, from its pre-Christian beginnings through its pivotal rôle in the story of Ireland's patron saint, Patrick, to its association with Irish politics.

A must for Irish and lovers of the Irish everywhere!

ISBN 0-86327-726-8

THE WOLFHOUND GUIDE TO
TEMPLE BAR

Kevin MacDermot

In recent years Dublin has become one of the most popular cities in Europe and the world for tourists of all ages, and Temple Bar has become the jewel in Dublin's crown.

Taking in the history and development of Temple Bar, this book is a guide to both the cultural and entertainment aspects of one of Europe's hottest tourist attractions. This is an indispensable guide for all visitors to Dublin.

Includes map, street guide, and information on shops, restaurants, pubs, clubs, galleries and accommodation in the area.

ISBN 0-86327-727-6